I Love My Rescue Dog

Stories That Will Warm Your Heart and Lift Your Spirit

By Terry Washington

Introduction

We love dogs. Don't we? And we love them a lot. They are part of our family and give us so much love and joy.

Warning: The stories in this e-book contain some material that may be disturbing to a younger audience. The dogs in these stories have experienced terrible situations before their rescues and have persevered.

According to the Humane Society's website (humanesociety.org):

"From 1970 to 2010, the number of dogs and cats in homes has increased from 67 million to an estimated 164 million. The annual number of dogs and cats euthanized in shelters has also decreased from 12–20 million to an estimated 3–4 million. However, there's still work to do: An estimated 2.7 million healthy shelter pets are not adopted each year, and only about 30 percent of pets in homes come from shelters and rescues."

Only approximately 20% of owned dogs are adopted from animal shelters. Sadly, due to the lack of awareness regarding spaying and neutering, the number of stray dogs is increasing each day. Many of these dogs go unwanted and are put down due to the lack of space in shelters and lack of available homes to take them in.

Most shelters and animal rights activists encourage people to adopt rather than breed or purchase dogs from pet stores to control this problem. But the rescue stories of these homeless dogs is not one sided. These animals have not only provided love and comfort to their owners, but at numerous times have returned the gesture by rescuing them too.

Heart Warming Dog Rescue Stories That Changed Lives

Despite these sad statistics, some dogs do find homes and families that love and nurture them. All rescue stories we hear are heart-warming, moving, and compelling. We may have adopted one of those dogs ourselves and know the love and joy that these furry friends bring to us. The following stories are examples of hope and love and proof that companionship and friendship comes in all sizes and forms. These are beautiful stories that will stir your heart's chords and dampen your eyes as you feel, hope, pray, and cheer for these animals and their rescuers.

Table of Contents

Introduction..2

Something Special..5

Rescue Me to Rescue You.............................9

Broken..12

Friendship to the Rescue.............................14

K-9 for the Rescue.......................................17

The Miracle of Life......................................19

No Room for Love..20

Julep Deserved to Live................................24

Don't Shop-Adopt!.......................................26

Something Special

Dixie had gotten used to the silence, just like most deaf dogs did, but things were supposed to get better after that, weren't they? Why was it that even after being homeless, hungry, and deaf she ended up with a broken leg and heartworms on a road with no help or support on the streets?

Sometimes things can only get better after being broken in more ways than can be easily fixed. And for Dixie, things were only getting worse. The cold winds were making her injured leg hurt a little more and the pangs of hunger along the deadly silence of her world was making her nervous and scared.

Dixie didn't know it yet, but help was on its way.

There were very few things Debra loved more than her seven adopted dogs including a cuddly, little deaf pit bull. It didn't matter that the puppy was deaf to Debra, her heart was a warm blanket for her foster dogs. Debra loved to help whenever she could, and in her spare time, she took in stray pups and helped find loving homes for them.

One morning she received a phone call a friend who knew that Debra took in strays. Her friend shared that a stray dog was found on a roadside. "The dog's hurt really bad, Debra, and she's deaf. She looks like she might be part lab. A real sweetheart, Debra. Black and brown. She needs someone to really care for her, and you were the first person I thought of. Can you take her?"

Debra felt instantly that there was something special about this dog and immediately felt a strong

5

connection to her. "Yes, of course I'll take her. I'll be right there," she replied with tears in her eyes imagining how lonely the dog must have been feeling on the streets.

Debra brought Dixie home and realized that one of Dixie's legs was horribly swollen. She rushed Dixie to the veterinarian worried about Dixie's health and if she was in pain. The vet said that Dixie's leg was badly shattered and had been for a long time. It needed to be amputated immediately. Debra started to cry and agreed to the surgery. She was going to make sure this dog survived and had a loving home to care for her no matter what.

Dixie wasn't sure what to make of all that was happening to her, she was in a room filled with posters of other dogs and a woman holding sharp tools. She touched Dixie's injured leg and Dixie cried out in pain. She wanted to run away. Dixie couldn't hear Debra's soothing words, but she felt Debra's warm arms around her and felt the care.

When Dixie woke up after the surgery, she felt warm and comfortable and her pain was almost gone. Maybe the pain was finally over. When Dixie realized she was missing her leg, she wasn't sure how to walk or if she could adjust. She didn't want to try to get up and Debra could tell that she felt sad. With a lot of encouragement and cuddling, Dixie started to try to walk again. This was a long and hard road for Dixie, but she had Debra right there guiding her along the way.

Dixie had to visit the veterinarian quite often for the surgery as well as for the extensive treatment for her heartworms. Although Dixie was learning to adjust with Debra, she had nightmares and was slow to trust Debra and the other dogs. But Debra's dogs were friendly, and they would cuddle with Dixie knowing that she had been through something horrible. They had warmed up to her quickly and cuddled with her often. It was like they understood what she had been through and could relate to her. They knew she needed love.

Debra reached out to the Little Pet Project and the Blind/Deaf Shelter Dog Networking group on her social network to help find a forever home for Dixie and to raise funds for her extensive medical procedures.

Dave and Clarissa were looking for a dog for their family. They had two young children and wanted to rescue a dog that needed a home. They found Dixie's pictures online and all four of them immediately fell in love with her. They had already rescued a pit bull named Suzi and they couldn't wait for Dixie to become a part of their family, too. They contacted Debra, and after four visits with Dixie, the family formally adopted her.

Dixie was sad that she had to leave Debra and her loving furry family. For the first time in her life she had found a home, a caring owner, and very loving and understanding companions. She didn't understand why she needed to leave. It seemed that good things never lasted long in her life anyway.

Dave and Clarissa's home proved to be the perfect place for Dixie eventually. Although she had difficulty adjusting to yet another new environment, she couldn't resist their warmth for long. When she snapped at Suzi, Suzi licked her on the ear. When

Dixie seemed to be struggling with her walking, the kids came over and hugged her and gave her treats. She was kept warm and was never left alone. Pretty soon she opened up and allowed herself to relax and be happy and loved.

Suzi would wake Dixie up when anyone called out her name, play with her, and even sleep and eat with her. In a very short time they became best friends.

Dixie had begun to feel content, safe, and happy. She no longer felt lonely and sad. Dave and Clarissa eventually trained Dixie to become a therapy dog, which allowed her to give and receive so much love in retirement homes and the children's wards at hospitals. She loved those visits and even though she couldn't hear the children's laughter when she jumped around and licked their sweet faces, she felt their strong love.

Rescue Me to Rescue You

Don was lying face down in the snow passed out. He was a 73-year-old retired police officer and a diabetic. His glucometer had recently failed resulting in sugar levels dropping so low that he passed out while on a nightly walk with his six-year-old terrier mix named Wyatt Earp.

Wyatt barked and jumped onto Don. He didn't know what to do! All he knew was that he needed to find help for his best friend, and he had to find it fast. Don had saved Wyatt's life a long time ago and it was time to do the same for him.

Wyatt still remembered the hardships he had faced before Don had come into his life five years ago. He remembered being caged in a shelter and waiting for a home day after day. People came in, looked around, and left without him. He wanted desperately to be picked up by one of those people and let out of his cage. He wanted to be played with and to run around.

One day Wyatt, along with a number of other dogs, was taken to an adoption event. Wyatt was excited by the change in scenery and all of the people walking around petting and holding dogs. Somebody would certainly find him adorable and offer him a proper home. As Wyatt sat there in his cage, his huge brown eyes were hopeful and excited.

As people poured into the Detroit Zoo adoption event in 2004, they roamed around to find the right companions. Most of them did, but sadly Wyatt wasn't one of those adopted as the event was starting coming to a close.

Don came to the event late as they were just about to start packing up for the day. He knew what he wanted. He was looking for a small dog to help him overcome the grief of losing his Yorkshire terrier when she died a couple of months ago. She had worked with Don for ten years in the police department, and Don missed her terribly and was still hurting.

As Don hurriedly roamed around the place, he couldn't find the right companion. "Maybe I'm not ready yet," he thought to himself sadly. Then he came face to face with Wyatt, who was looking at him with big, brown, pleading eyes. Don's heart started to beat a little faster thinking of taking this pup home, but he moved on past the cage. He wasn't looking for a terrier mix. He needed a smaller dog!

Don kept walking but couldn't stop thinking about Wyatt. When he looked back at Wyatt's cage, Wyatt was still looking at him. Don laughed and walked back over to the cage. At that moment knew that he had no choice. "Looks like you're coming home with me little guy. I couldn't resist those eyes of yours," Don said in a soft voice. Wyatt understood and excitedly barked his agreement.

Don had not only opened his home to Wyatt, but also his heart. The two had soon developed a strong bond and were inseparable. The long walks that they took together each night did wonders for both. Wyatt experienced freedom and companionship, while Don's doctor claimed he had a perfect EKG, even after two heart attacks and several stents! Don's doctor shared that he believed the dog was saving his life one walk at a time. Don knew this was true and loved Wyatt unconditionally.

10

But today, Don was passed out and in danger, and Wyatt knew he had to do something soon to save his dear friend's life. He ran to the corner of the street, a five-lane highway, and started barking incessantly. Wyatt made sure he was under a streetlight so that people could notice him in the dark of the night.

Shortly Marjorie, one of Don's neighbors, came out of her house to see what was going on and instantly recognized Wyatt. Marjorie knew something was wrong the way Wyatt was barking and came running. "What's going on little one? Where's Don?" Wyatt led her to where Don was lying and she gasped. She took out her cell phone and called for help immediately. Don was rushed to the hospital.

Marjorie shared with the emergency team and the doctors how important Wyatt was to Don and Wyatt was allowed to stay with Don while he was in a coma. Wyatt slept by Don's side for the entire time. The nurses brought him food and even took him for a walk outside every so often. They were touched that Wyatt was so committed to Don and gave Wyatt his own pillow to sleep on if he wanted it.

After being in a coma for 18 hours, Don pulled through. The doctors told Don that he had a very close call with death. Just another 10 to 15-minute delay in getting help would have meant a completely different and deadly outcome for Don.

Don knew that Wyatt had saved his life this time and was grateful to his little buddy. He also knew how this dog had saved his life every step of the way since they adopted each other.

Broken

In the lively city of Bogota, Colombia, lived Lucy, an American Staffordshire Terrier. She was medium height with a beautiful, golden brown coat. Lucy had deep inquisitive eyes, a mellow temperament, and a desire to be loved. Lucy also had a broken nose, a disfigured jaw and a broken heart.

Each day Lucy would wake up to more excruciating pain than what she had endured the day before. Lucy was used as a submissive dog to train fighting dogs for aggression. Each of Lucy's days was spent being torn apart bit by bit. There was no end to her agony. When she wasn't being attacked by other dogs, she was being used for repeated mating with male dogs.

There was a time early on when Lucy would fight off those attacks. But her owner had put a stop to that by pulling out some of her canine teeth. She no longer fought or even resisted the cruelty that she was exposed to each day, she had accepted it, and lived with it.

She didn't know who to blame, the animals that caused the pain or the humans that trained them for it. Either way, nobody came to her rescue. And chances were that nobody ever would.

One day Lucy decided she had had enough. She knew she wasn't strong enough to fight her oppressors, but she could escape from the daily abuse. Her oppressors had underestimated Lucy's drive to live and left her untied in the yard. And so, she made her escape one night in the darkness. She had escaped successfully, but she had a long road ahead of her.

Lucy found herself on the streets pregnant and emaciated. Each day, she felt herself becoming weaker and weaker. Not only in her body, but in her heart as well. She did her best to live until finally help arrived.

A man driving by saw Lucy on the street left for dead. She was badly bruised, battered, and deformed. He grabbed an old towel he had in his truck to wrap around her and drove her to a local veterinarian hospital. The vet examined her and found out that along with her broken nose, jaw, and bites and bruises, her uterus was twisted. This was Lucy's sixth pregnancy, and in her condition, she wouldn't survive through it. The vet's choice was to either save the babies or Lucy, and he chose to save Lucy.

Lucy stayed in a loving foster home for six months in Bogota, as she slowly recovered, until the Stray From the Heart Foundation took up her case to find her a forever home.

Stray From the Heart, a volunteer-driven organization that rescues abused and homeless dogs, found out about Lucy through their network. They were so moved by her story and arranged to have Lucy flown to New York to help her find a permanent secure home, which they eventually did.

Today, Lucy's broken jaw and nose make up her individual character, a reminder of a past that is long behind her. Lucy is neither bitter nor angry about what happened in her past. She is happy and content with the comfort that her new family provides her. She likes to laze around on the sofa all day and allow her loving family to spoil and pamper her day after day.

Friendship to the Rescue

Bobbie the pug didn't know what was going on. Everyone in the house was frantically running around the house. Her family was busy packing away bags and emergency food supplies. She followed them around, but nobody paid any attention to her. Bob Cat, her blind little friend, was just as confused as Bobbie.

Both of them sat down in a corner and waited for the commotion to come to an end to find out what was going on.

"I am sure it's not a hurricane. They are just overreacting!" said the father of the house.

"Katrina is coming, and it's best to leave now rather than getting caught up in it," the mother replied.

Bobbie was confused, but recognized packing for a road trip when she saw it and it sounded like a lot of fun. It had been a long time since the whole family had taken a vacation together. Bobbie and Bob Cat were both excited. Now, all they had to do was just behave themselves until the family prepared for the trip.

Finally the preparations were over. Bobbie started wagging his tail in excitement. The father placed a leash on her, took her outside, and shut the door on their way out with Bob Cat locked inside. Bobbie kept trying to look behind her to see why Bob Cat wasn't going with them.

Then all of a sudden Bobbie was tied to the porch with a bowl of food and water in front of her. The family drove off. She was confused. They never left her tied up on the porch before. Hours passed and no one came.

Night soon fell and Bobbie realized that her family was not coming back as she saw dozens of cars packed with families leaving the city. Some of these families had their pets safely tucked in their cars. But not Bobbie and Bob Cat. They had been left behind to weather a terrible storm and Bobbie was scared.

As Bobbie lied down on the ground, she thought about Bob Cat and wondered if he knew what was going on? She heard a noise coming from the house as Bob Cat made it out of the cat door from the kitchen. Bobbie barked to Bob Cat so that he could find his way to her. He nuzzled next to her and they both went to sleep.

Next morning they woke up with determination to take care of each other. Bobbie managed to chew her way out of the leash on the porch and both of them wandered around the empty streets. They tried to find food and shelter as best they could with Bob Cat taking Bobbie's lead. They stuck together as days and nights passed away with no sign of help.

As the roaring storm named Katrina violently took over New Orleans, Bobbie and Bob Cat did their best to snuggled into a small box for cover. They spent four months on the street hungry, afraid, and hoping that their family would come to rescue them. But they also strengthened their loving for each other and their trust in one another during that time.

And one day, help did arrived. Not from their owners but from a rescue team scouting for lost pets in New Orleans.

The rescue team placed Bobbie in her own cage at first but she was terrified of being separated from Bob Cat. She howled and howled until the team finally understood and placed Bob Cat in the cage with her. Seeing how close the dog and cat were to each other, the rescue team sent Bobbie and Bob Cat to Best Friends Animal Sanctuary so that the organization could find a home that would adopt them together.

The two were soon adopted by a loving couple on a ranch in Oregon. They settled in quickly and became attached to the couple who loved them just as much. Sadly Bob Cat, who had gotten very sick after being on the street for so long wasn't able to survive for long after being adopted and passed away. Bobbie may have found a new home, but she lost a true friend and companion.

The pug grieved for Bob Cat and with the help of her adopted family, she led a full life of comfort, warmth, and loving.

K-9 for the Rescue

K-9 dogs are specially trained to detect trouble to help control terrorism, drug trafficking, and even for rescue purposes. K-9s, like most of our security services, wear the honor of protecting the country with pride.

Dino, a regal German Shepherd, was no different. He worked with the Greensboro Police Department as a drug dog. He was courageous, intelligent, and very proud to be able to serve his country. Dino had assisted in many drug raids and was always very successful. He finally had to retire in 2012 due to his advancing age.

Dino's handler gave him away to his neighbor for adoption, which was surprising to Dino. The German Shepherd had always expected his handler to take care of him as he aged, and he didn't like his new owner or the small room he now had to live in. He was only taken out for five-minute walks twice a day, and he didn't really get any other activity. Although Dino was getting older, he was used to being active and wanted to run and play in the yard.

As days passed by, Dino eventually learned to adjust in his new home. He saw his handler sometimes when taken out for walks, but his handler had clearly moved on. He wouldn't really acknowledge Dino in a loving way and only heartlessly pat Dino's head whenever the two neighbors bumped into each other on one of their short walks.

Dino was sad. He missed being in the police quarters and being with everyone he knew. He sometimes cried and his new owner became upset with him frequently. One day, Dino's new owner took him out for a ride and dropped him off at an animal control facility.

Soon Dino found himself in a cage surrounded by other dogs that had no families or homes to go back to. Each day many of the dogs left to never return, while many more new dogs were brought in to fill the cages. Dino knew he didn't have long to live. He had always expected to be loved and respected, that his loyalty and dedication would be rewarded.

A rescue organization soon found out about Dino through a friend of the neighbor's and immediately took action. After a lot of red tape, the rescue organization was able to get Dino out of the facility and place him with a woman living alone and who always wanted a dog to care for. Dino fell in love with her and took care for her as much as she cared for him.

Dino is now eleven years old and with time is losing his hearing, but he has been honored with a secure home and someone to love him just as he deserves.

The Miracle of Life

Daniel Miladro was no ordinary dog. This stray beagle mix went through some ups and many downs before he earned the name of Daniel Miladro. Yes, he has earned his name through his own bravery, resilience, and perhaps a bit of angelic assistance. He was honored the name Daniel in relation to the Biblical figure who had come out of the lion's den unscathed. And his last name, Miladro is Spanish for miracle, which is what this wonder dog experienced.

Daniel was just like any other stray dog trying to make it through the day, wandering the streets, and avoiding the animal control teams. Life was hard for him, as was for most of his canine friends, many of which were caught and euthanized by the animal control teams.

When he was about six months old, Daniel too was found and taken to an animal shelter. He knew he wouldn't be going back to the streets. Daniel was energetic and friendly. He soon made friends with other dogs at the shelter until they were taken away and never returned.

One day Daniel, along with 17 other dogs, was taken out of his cage and taken to another place. Daniel knew he wouldn't be coming back to the cage, just like none of his friends did.

Daniel was placed in a stainless-steel room the size of a pickup truck with the other dogs and the door was closed. The box was dark and he couldn't see anything or anybody around him. He started barking along with the other dogs. They could all tell something bad was going to happen. Daniel heard strange noises coming from the vents in the room. Soon all the barking subsided and then Daniel heard only a few whimpers. These also stopped after a few minutes.

Finally the door to the stainless-steel room, which had been filled with carbon monoxide, was opened. The animal control team saw seventeen dogs lying dead on the floor, but Daniel was alive and well looking at them scared and confused. The team was shocked and gave the miracle dog the name Daniel Miladro. After a thorough examination, the vet claimed that he hadn't suffered any internal injuries and shared in his own words, "It was like something or 'someone' was protecting him."

The news of this dog's miraculous survival soon made it into the local newspapers and within days hundreds of people contacted the shelter wishing to adopt Daniel.

A man named Joe who lived in Nutley, New Jersey, was finally chosen as Daniel's guardian. Today Daniel lives happily with his new family.

Daniel not only miraculously survived the euthanization, but his experience also opened debates about inhumane forms of euthanasia in animal shelters. Sadly Daniel's recovery however did not change the fate of the other dogs who passed away on that day and each day following.

No Room for Love

Sam was a graphic designer living alone in Liberty, Missouri, and adopted Milo when the Labrador was only six months old. The two soon became best friends. They spent almost all of Sam's free time together. They played with each other, went for long walks, and even ate together.

Sam always shared his secrets with Milo, his heartbreaks and his loneliness. Whenever Sam brought a girlfriend over, they ended up playing with Milo until Milo was finally tucked into bed. Sam always brought Milo with him to visit Sam's parents in Kansas City every Christmas. They were a happy family of two.

Sam eventually married a wonderful woman. Milo was excited to have another person to play with. The problem was that Sam's wife wasn't very fond of Milo and didn't want to spend much time with him. Slowly Sam started spending less and less time with Milo. Most of his days were spent being ignored or on his own, and when Sam had a baby boy named Alex, he was really ignored.

Apart from the necessary duties like feeding, walking, and the vet appointments Sam had almost no time for Milo. It had been years since Milo and Sam spent any real time together and Milo had become depressed.

As young Alex grew older things changed though. Milo and Alex became best friends, and it was like the old days had returned. Although Milo did not have the same energy as before, he loved playing with Alex and life was good again. They played in the yard, took long walks, and slept together in Alex's bed. Milo loved Alex.

When Alex was six years old, Sam and his wife made the decision to move to Los Angeles. Sam decided it was time for the family to move on to bigger and better opportunities.

They found a beautiful apartment in Los Angeles in a safe area with good schools, parks, and recreational centers. There was only one problem. The building they were moving into had a very strict No-Pet policy. Milo was 14 by that time and Sam thought he was much too old to drag along across the country anyway.

Sam and Alex headed to the local animal shelter with Milo. Alex didn't realize what was going on until Sam asked Alex to say goodbye to Milo. Alex cried and hugged Milo so tightly and refused to let go. Sam had to pull the crying Alex away from Milo.

Sam didn't even say goodbye to Milo. He couldn't look in his eyes and he felt bad about what was happening. Milo sadly watched as Sam led Alex out of the shelter and left him there in that strange place. He was used to confinement, but he wasn't used to being caged with other animals. Milo just wanted to cuddle next to Alex, to play with him and let him tickle his paws. He missed home very badly.

Luckily Milo was soon adopted by Watson, a wounded army officer just back from the Iraqi war. They were both hurting and learned to be vulnerable with each other and trust each other. Life for Milo became whole again. He knew how to be loyal and offer comfort, and Watson offered the same respect and companionship in return. Together they healed.

Julep Deserved to Live

Julep was a lively collie puppy. She and the rest of her siblings had been given away as presents after being born. Julep was given to a family of four living in Alabama. Julep was excited to make new friends and had a lot of energy. Her new family wasn't quite sure how to handle a puppy, and at times an entire day would go by before they offered her any food. Hardly anyone ever played with her.

But Julep remained jolly. She played with shoelaces or the empty food boxes that were always lying around the house. She didn't understand why no one would play with her. She wagged her tail and jumped on the kids so that they could notice her and play with her, but they were not interested.

One day, the father of the family brought home a cage and locked Julep inside. The cage was only big enough to stand up in but not big enough to play in, not that there was ever anything to play with. Days went by and Julep just sat there staring at the walls of the empty room that they had placed her cage in.

Julep's health, along with her spirit kept on suffering with each passing day. The cage had become too small for her. She could hardly sit properly in it, but no one cared. Julep didn't know what to hope for.

Julep was hardly fed, only rarely taken out of the cage, and even rarer still given any attention. Julep had been mated several times and had delivered multiple litters. This only made her weaker. Julep just lived from one day to the next hoping things would get better.

When Julep was about four or five years old (no one was really keeping track) the father took her out for a drive. He stopped the car in the middle of a quiet, secluded road. He led Julep out of the car and shot her in the head. He drove off leaving Julep to die.

Fortunately, an elderly woman and her adult daughter drove by soon thereafter and found Julep on the road. They saw that the collie was still breathing and rushed her to the animal hospital. Julep had emergency surgery to save her. The vet also discovered that Julep's muscles were atrophied due to cage confinement and lack of use. Julep wasn't able to walk for more than a few steps before needing to lay down to rest. Julep was also suffering from mange, which hadn't been treated for a very long time, and the gunshot to her head had left her partially blind. Although there were chances that her vision might return, the chances were very small.

Julep was transferred to the Wolf's Arkansas Sanctuary where she gradually recovered. Julep had not experienced what kindness and compassion felt like, but things had changed since she was rescued.

Julep's previous family abandoning her was a blessing in disguise. Julep's health and her spirits healed with time. She was beginning see more, play, and even love again!

Don't Shop-Adopt!

Stray dogs are put down all year round - even on Christmas day. And although hundreds of people line up to adopt dogs like Daniel Miladro, not many people are willing to do the same for other dogs. Neutering and spaying dogs is pivotal to controlling the overall problem of overpopulation among dogs on the streets.

These are only some of the heartwarming successful dog stories, and there are plenty of others with more being written every day.

We can all make a big difference by adopting dogs from shelters rather than buying them from breeders or pet stores. Approximately 25 percent of the dogs in shelters are pure breeds. So the next time you go out looking for presents, companionship, or a dose of animal love don't forget to pay a visit to your local shelter and save a life!

These stories, just like many others, have not only changed the lives of the dogs, but also of the people and families that have adopted them. These stories would not be possible if it were not for the courageous men and women who rescue dogs providing safety and shelter and love for these lost souls.

Dogs are one of the most compassionate, loving, and, of course, loyal companions and by offering love and care, you can get all the perks of such a special bond too!

Made in the USA
Lexington, KY
06 December 2014